Patchworks

By

Barbara Towell

Patchworks
By Barbara Towell

Spinetinglers Elite Publishing
22 Vestry Road
Co. Down
BT23 6HJ
UK

www.spinetinglerspublishing.com

This edition published by Spinetinglers Elite Publishing 2014

ISBN 978-1-906657-18-5

For my husband John, my family, friends and all who inspired this collection of poems.

Patchworks Foreword

The poetry in this anthology represents the myriad of reflections and experiences I have encountered during my life. Hence the title Patchworks.

It will come as no surprise to realise some of the poems here were inspired by real situations and people, whereas others were written whilst writing alongside my students or those I led in creative writing workshops. I have also included the verse written as a preface for my novel "A Little Piece for Mother" and the poem "The Real Me" which was commissioned.

I hope you will enjoy these few patches from my life.

Barbara Towell

I Hate Sundays

I hate Sundays.
A single mother
All alone.
Mountains of washing piling high.
The washing machine breaks down.
I hate Sundays.
Families on TV laugh and go for picnics.
All alone
Except for the screeches
Of fighting Kids
Who long for their father instead of me,
I long for Monday
When I am needed.
Needed to nurse the terminal patients
On my hospital ward.

Eastbourne – a special day

(This poem relates to a true incident from my childhood. Even now when I recall the event, I experience the same vivid emotions of that day.)

Eastbourne.
I'm six;
Small for my age.
Leap from breakwater.
Shallow side to deep waves.

Plunging down,
Rolling -
Swirl into a grave
Of white fizzing bubbles
And tiny sand grains.
They surge past my eyes
Which register
Death.
It's on the horizon
Stealing my breath.

The rush of cold water
Stifles my screams.
I gulp like a fish
I'm drowning -
No dream!
I just cannot swim.
I try as I may
Soon I'll be...
Nothing.
Life lost in a day.
A day which I'd long for.

The sea my old friend;
Betraying my friendship.
My life It will end.

Those words of my mother, still echo ‘cross time,
“Don’t go back in the water, now that you’re dry.”
And what was my question in the face of death’s cry?
Would anyone miss me? -
Disobedient child.

Too late to heed warnings.
The water’s too deep.
Can’t swim,
Only splash.
Flay arms,
Kick feet.

Only by fortune
The break it came near.
I clutched and I hugged it
Strength in my fear.
I hauled myself up.
I threw myself down
Ran to the pebbles,
Felt my heart pound.
Sat in the aftermath
Seaweed my crown.

Nobody noticed,
Nobody knew
Why me, that small girl
Sat sobbing and blue.

Eastbourne,

I'm six;
Small for my age.
Disobedient child,
Alone and afraid.
I never did tell,
How on that day
My death came so close;
A whisker away.

And now decades later
Those photographed smiles
Remind me, my children
May not have had lives.
I'm reminded how death is a hair's breadth away
As was for a child in Eastbourne that day.

Autumn

Say farewell to life
And summer song
As the russet leaves fall,
Wither to a shadeless beige;
Metamorphosise into layers
Of dying.
The wild wind
Through the forest
Blows a winter prelude
Whilst fractured light
Peeps through branches of naked oaks,
Polishing their rich brown fruit.
Conkers lie in the shadow of age-old trunks,
Waiting to be some small child's treasure.
Birdsong heralds the season's change,
Squirrels secrete their acorn cache while
Hedgehogs nose and mutter their way
To cosy sleep
With dreams of worms, slugs and April days.

Tunes of autumn,
Soon to be replaced
By the music of winter.

Left from Life

A golden teddy with one amber eye
Flops in the attic where spider webs lie.
Beams through cracked windows
Turn vases to jewels,
Crystals from glass bowls
Worth a penny or two.
The looking-glass aches
For a face to reflect,
But all of these items are
Simply rejects.
The house it stands empty
In layers of dust
Home to the mice;
And smelling of must.
Things loved and cherished
Once part of each day
Lie damaged, forgotten,
In this house up for sale.

The Real Me

Who asks the questions? Who then replies?
Who hides behind that mask repeating daily lies?
Watch the door open, who will emerge?
Is it you? Is it me, with a ghost of a smile?

Is it really you, a photo in the dark?
Lurking in the shadows, playing in the park?
Listen to the echoes of laughter far away.
Is it you? No, it's me, that child of yesterday.

Hidden places, solid masks which
plaster over years,
Changing photos into prints, or
negatives of fear.
Can the real me stand up alone and
touch the world outside?
A joyful clown of make-believe,
chained, heavily disguised.

Think about the candle burning in
the night,
When princesses and junkies die
equal in His sight.
A flame of life denied its breath
when only God can see
What's hidden in between the layers
of "the real me".

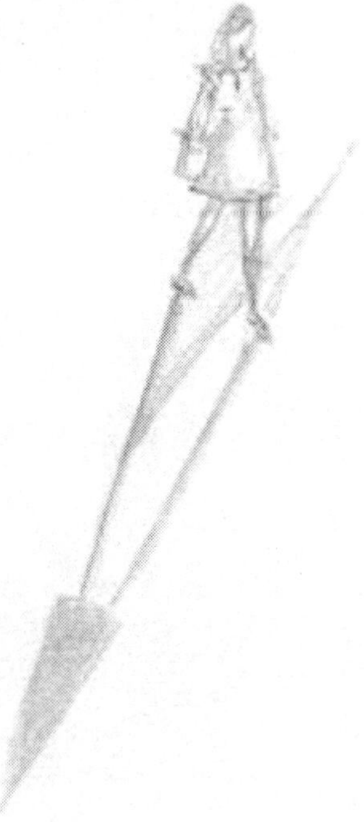

October Storm

Half-baked leaves of gold, red and brown
Swirl in maelstroms. Endless circles
Caught in the breath of a storm.
The wild dancing wind carries angry warnings whilst
Phantom voices haunt the sleepless dawn,
Trading gentle October whispers for
Voices of savage waves.

The sky cracks into cloud and rain.
Shivers of mist cloak path and pond.
Trees bow, branches bend
And sweep the shaking lawn whilst
Night's veil lifts to a pale morning grey.
Mother Nature stirs and paints a
Splash of waltzing colours on this autumn day.

Sorry My Darling

Sorry my darling.
I forgot to video "Startrek"
But I was playing my guitar –
Singing the song that you wrote!

Sorry my darling.
I forgot to make the Bolognese sauce,
But I was practising for the gig –
The best song that you've ever written!

Sorry my darling.
Hope you don't mind
A take-a-way pizza tonight – again -
In front of last night's episode of "Startrek"!

A Smile

A smile freely given is a gift like no other.

Given in the early morning light to the homeless man
Who blinks his way to a sobering day.

Given to the frail ninety year old at the supermarket
Who struggles to keep herself out of the old people's home.

Given to the mum whose autistic child simply cannot behave.
Feels unwelcome in our world of "normality"- alone, ashamed.

Given to the widowed neighbour who braves each hour
Knowing that life will never be the same.

Given to the unpopular, hard-faced boss who carries the can.
The sick, the rejected, the angered and those unjustly framed.

A smile. It costs nothing – yet is everything.
In that fleeting moment, it can change
A heart, a day, a lifetime.
It is a blessing.
A free gift like no other.

If the Birds Still come to the Garden

He asks me if the birds still come to the garden.
Home, already seems a distant past.
Lying beneath the crisp, ivory sheets of another world
He chases the memories - only a day away.

Life's pages turn.
Keep turning
Towards the moment when his life will be but history.

Far below the hospital ward
Fireworks dance, crackle and play;
And he asks, if I remembered to keep the cat inside today.
A rocket, like a stretched
out candle flame
Squeals across the Guy
Fawkes sky.
I nod my head, hold back
the tears.
He smiles. I sigh.

Outside, the night's alive
with golden flakes.
He shuts his eyes. His voice
fades as he asks again,
If the birds still come to
the garden;
And slips away.

I like Friday Best

I like Friday best!
I feel the lazy weekend approach,
The days of endless bedclothes and eleven o'clock curry.
Newspapers and easy yawns.
Shut-eye at dawn.
Lolling on the puffed up sofa to the afternoon sport -
On TV of course!
Novels and crisps,
Nachos and dips to
Classic FM with the sounds of the hoover;
And of course the promise of a pint, or ten - after midnight.
Yes I like Friday best.

Let's blot out
Monday,
Tuesday,
Wednesday,
Even Thursday.
The working week remains a
Blank in the diary
As we stumble aimlessly through one day to the next,
One week to the next,
One year to the next
Wishing our lives away.

Then, death's on the horizon,
And we long for
Monday,
Tuesday,
Wednesday,

Thursday,
Even working-day Friday,
And hate the approach of that endless, lazy weekend.

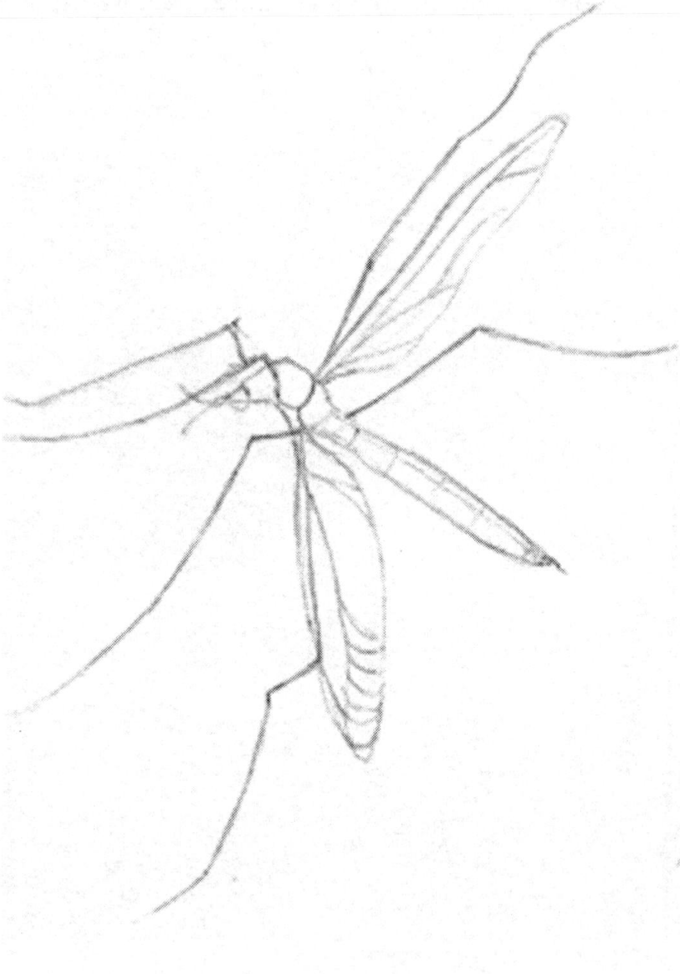

Daddy-longlegs

I used to quite like
Daddy-longlegs.
Their rice paper wings.
Their bent cotton legs.

Whispering the promise of winter,
They'd hover in corners
Of evening rooms.
Shiver in halos of light;
Until at last, exhausted and
Longing for freedom,
They'd battle with glass
Or a door closed behind them.
Carefully ,
Cupping soft hands
I'd make a safe cage.
Carry them gently,
Twitching in my palms
To a half opened window,
And watch them fly into the night.

That is until...
Someone told me -
They are really spiders with wings.
Now...

I can't tolerate being in the same room as one!

Whiskey

Our tight ball of meow,
Dominates the double bed;
Pristine white and ebony.
We know our place -
Lying on each edge.
He stretches wide,
Flicks crookéd tail.
My sleepy hand
Strokes silken head –
Again - and again.
Gold marble eyes
Shine. He's wide awake,
Watching mine
Pretending sleep.
But he's no fool.

4am.

Our fur king stands
Velvets his paws,
Treads the duvet
As if thro' snow.
Whisker-pad meets cheek.
A breathing cuddly toy, he drops,
Flops into a feline heap
His perfect head
Cupped in my hand,
He drifts back to sleep.
I lie awake recalling
A stray: black smudge on face.
Oil painted belly,
Hungry eyes. Rib thin.

Wild. Afraid.

A cat with no name,
Pushed himself
Into our lives and
Thankfully -
Stayed.

Jealousy

A frozen, tight smile
With distant eyes roam the corners of the room;
Afraid of what they may see.
Ears alive, alert for
Chilly whispers over coffee cups which may
Haunt her dreams
And twist them into nightmares.

She stares out of the window,
Chilly and shrinking
As she pictures the enemy;
The shadows outside,
Creeping towards her.

She sits in her smart navy blue.
Listens. Warms to the praise
That was not meant for her.
Glows in false glory
As she bridles and sweetly says, "Thank you."
And dares not look at me.

Dawning

The kettle purrs in the kitchen below
Whilst upstairs the cat nips my fingers awake.
The buzz of a bee nuzzles the shade
Breaking through zones where dreams meet day.

A whisker of light,
A whisper of dawn.
Trains in the distance,
An intrusive alarm.

I leap up in horror
Fearing I'm late.
It's gone 7.30!
Work at 8?

Dressed, in the bathroom brushing my teeth.
The kettle still purring, the cat at my feet.
Then I remember –

It's my day off!

Nothing Changes

Cherry blossom burning as it glides on the rain.
Wheels are always turning, but they come back again.
People always dying alone with decay.
Ask yourself a question -
Do you change from day to day?

Sand grains getting smaller as they're tossed by the sea.
Mankind always searching as it longs to be free.
Children always crying with the world's sordid ways.
Ask yourself a question –
Do you change from day to day?

'Cause time goes on - and on and on
'Cause time goes on – and on and on -
And centuries pass.

Sugar turning bitter as it's bitten by the spice.
Living is a gamble, so why not throw the dice?
And hope the even numbers tumble while you play.
Ask yourself a question –
Do you change from day to day?

Rays from a prism darken losing light.
The summer of a lifetime is captured in the night,
Taken to a graveyard, where no one can say:
Ask yourself a question –
Do you change from day to day?

’Cause time goes on – and on and on
’Cause time goes on - and on and on –
And centuries pass...

But nothing changes.

Reflection on your Dying

(In memory of Dr. Ladislav Fisch - my father)

A moment each day
My heart stops for just a little while
As I recall your touch,
Your hand reaching out to take mine
In your last hours of life.
Your brown eyes filled with warmth
Still full of vitality
Meeting mine to say a silent
Unrequited goodbye which
You just could not voice.
Yet those silent words spoke everything
And more, that last time
As your frail body, yet sharp mind
Asked for the peace and dignity to die alone.

A moment each day
My heart stops for just a little while
As I wonder at your parting,
Your lone passage as you
Lay between the crisp white hospital
linen with
Panoramic London, your refuge,
stretched before you.
You left
With no one, no one
You loved by your side.

Did you die alone, for you?
Or for those of us you leave behind?
Was it to make the loss
We feel for you
Just that little bit easier?

Masks

(Foreword from my novel "A Little Piece for Mother")

The mask begins to crack and the shadows creep
through the fractures like tiny beads of blood,
seeping from an untended wound. It happens so
slowly that no one notices until the mask shatters
to reveal a monster too dark to defeat.

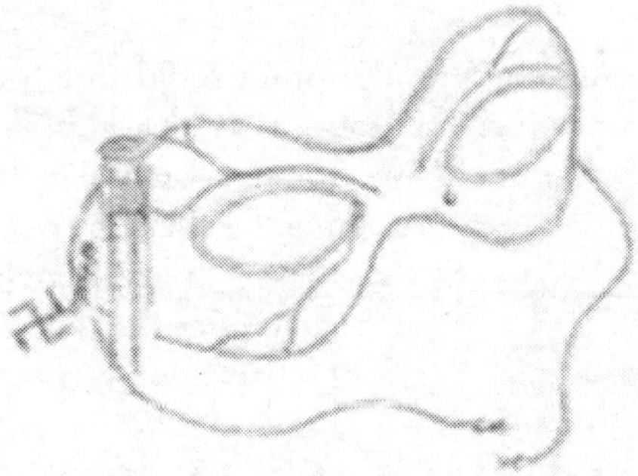

Childhood Mother

My childhood mother sings as she hands me a towel after bath time.
She's there in the kitchen looking out of the window humming
While she cuts up fish for our cats.
She's perched on the edge of my bed, reading "Winnie the Pooh" and "Brer Rabbit".
Frying potatoes 'til they're crisp and brown.
She spoons out jelly for Sunday tea,
Amusingly, calling it plastic.

My childhood mother scolds me for creeping inside the larder
Before the house is awake, gobbling up all the Milky Ways.
She scolds me for stealing apples from our neighbour's tree.
For chucking the sour ones over the fence.
She's aghast – angry - catching me stick gum
Under the pew at mass.
Sadly, that Sunday, no sweets for me.

The memory of my childhood mother remains
A patchwork quilt –
Squares bright,
Squares grey.
Half-remembered days
Of laughter
And shame
Recalled in pale shades,
In that photo frame
Of my life.

Hillingdon

I wonder what the soldiers of World War Two would say
Returning to the battlefield of Hillingdon today?
Owls, are they hooting?
No, it's the honking of a car.
Cries of bombed out victims?
No, just shrieking from a bar.
Yet the grass is always greener
On the other side
Whether 'cross boundaries of nations
Or that barrier of time.

Lord of Darkness – My Prayer

Yes, triumph!
I am winning the contest that began in the Garden of Eden with
God; those Gods who are put on a pedestal …
Put themselves on a pedestal.

Great – a war in Syria!
Let's hope Korea builds nuclear weapons….
Go on kill a few more billions.
Hitler. Stalin. Saddam Hussain.
Have a little patience …
And they'll create more the same.

I hear the whisper of a changing prayer
Evermore on the human lip….

"Lord of Darkness,
Who art in Hell
Your name shall be adored.
Thy kingdom come.
Thy will be done
On Earth as it is in Hell…"

Yes, yes!

"Give us this day
Our daily dose of violence
And forgive those who fail to murder and steal,
And lead us into temptation.
For thine, dearest Satan, is the power and the glory…"

Yes, Yes!

"For ever and ever, and ever and ever and ever…"

Believe it...
Newspapers, my witness - it is MY day now…

"AMEN!"

God's Proclamation

Men you have failed!
Look at the catastrophe you have created upon
My Earth,
The one that I made for you to enjoy!
The wars, the pollution, not to mention the hatred.
It's all down to you;
And you have the cheek to blame it on Eve.
For, you accuse her of corrupting man - and what?
Leading man to temptation.
An apple, a mere apple was stolen!
I think it is time to stop casting the blame.
I think it is time to give up your reign.
Take a back seat;
Leave it to women.
The "weaker sex?" Ha ha!
You've had your chance –
Your era – sorry eras – have passed.
The time has come to snuff you out.
You're superfluous!
In fact
You are the weakest link!
Goodbye!

The Nobody Child

You look at me with fire in your smile,
Yet all I want is to help you.
A raised fist flickers in your eye.
Blink.

Knuckles poised above your bleeding lid.
Half a woman - unruly chestnut hair
Pale like a bone, with a split lip.
A grimace filled with hatred.

Hunched in the corner,
A mane of greasy locks
Frames the hungry stare.
Retreating, hunted, your shrill howl fills the air
As you struggle to separate me
From him
And me from her.

Silence speaks.
Baffled.
My hand outreached
Haunts you as you creep away
Expecting it to knock you into next week;
Knock you into the nobody
You recognise in the mirror each day.

You look at me with ice in your smile.
But I cannot erase the years,
Only try,
To crack that barrier;
Help you child,

Through the journey of life.

Acknowledgements

A big thank you to my husband John who gives me endless encouragement. Thank you to Lauren Neill for believing in me and Hannah Fox at Spinetinglers Elite for her hard work on my behalf plus my literary agent, Jodi Dougan for her constant support.

I feel Swakeleys High School in Hillingdon deserves a mention and thank you. It was during the many happy years teaching English there, that many of these poems were written.

A massive thank you to Mary Linkie for the wonderful drawings which illustrate my poems perfectly.

About the Author

Barbara Towell lives with her husband and cat in North West London where she works as an English teacher and author. 'Patchworks' is her first poetry anthology, but her novel 'A Little Piece for Mother' is also published by Spinetinglers Elite. In addition, Barbara writes short stories, scripts and songs and has had articles published in national magazines. In 2013 she was the winner of the Harrow Libraries' Crime Writing Competition and the musical, 'Faith is the Key' which she co-wrote with her husband, was staged during the spring at the Dumfries Festival in Scotland

Lightning Source UK Ltd.
Milton Keynes UK
UKOW05f0055180614

233639UK00001B/1/P

9 781906 657185